Butterfly
Effect

The National Poetry Series

The National Poetry Series was established in 1978 to ensure the publication of five poetry collections annually through participating publishers. Publication is funded by James A. Michener, the Copernicus Society of America, Edward J. Piszek, the Lannan Foundation, and the Tiny Tiger Foundation.

1998 Competition Winners

Rigoberto González
So Often the Pitcher Goes to Water Until It Breaks
Chosen by Ai
Published by University of Illinois Press

Harry Humes
Butterfly Effect
Chosen by Pattiann Rogers
Published by Milkweed Editions

Joan Murray
Looking For the Parade
Chosen by Robert Bly
Published by W. W. Norton

Ed Roberson
Atmosphere Conditions
Chosen by Nathaniel Mackey
Published by Sun & Moon Press

Lee Ann Roripaugh
Heart Mountain
Chosen by Ishmael Reed
Published by Viking Penguin

Butterfly Effect

Harry Humes

MILKWEED EDITIONS

Distributed by Publishers Group West
Published 1999 by Milkweed Editions
Printed in the United States of America
Cover design by Wesley B. Tanner
Cover painting, "Out the Window on the Truck Fossil," by Michael K. Paxton, courtesy of Byron Roche Gallery, Chicago
Interior design by Donna Burch
The text of this book is set in Sabon
99 00 01 02 03 5 4 3 2 1
First Edition

Milkweed Editions, a nonprofit publisher, gratefully acknowledges support from the Elmer L. and Eleanor J. Andersen Foundation; James Ford Bell Foundation; Bush Foundation; Dayton Hudson Foundation on behalf of Dayton's, Mervyn's California, and Target Stores; Doherty, Rumble & Butler Foundation; Honeywell Foundation; McKnight Foundation; Minnesota State Arts Board through an appropriation by the Minnesota State Legislature; Norwest Foundation on behalf of Norwest Bank Minnesota; Lawrence and Elizabeth Ann O'Shaughnessy Charitable Income Trust in honor of Lawrence M. O'Shaughnessy; Oswald Family Foundation; Ritz Foundation on behalf of Mr. and Mrs. E. J. Phelps Jr.; John and Beverly Rollwagen Fund of the Minneapolis Foundation; St. Paul Companies, Inc.; Star Tribune Foundation; U. S. Bancorp Piper Jaffray Foundation on behalf of U. S. Bancorp Piper Jaffray; and the support of generous individuals.

Library of Congress Cataloging-in-Publication Data
Humes, Harry.
    Butterfly effect / Harry Humes. — 1st ed.
      p.   cm.
    ISBN 1-57131-408-3 (pbk.)
    I. Title.
PS3558.U444B88   1999
811'.54—dc21   98-32216
                                            CIP

For my wife, Nancy,
my daughters Leah and Rachel,
and my family, past and present

Acknowledgments

Defined Providence, "Ax Heads"

Gettysburg Review, "Owl Call," "Grizzly Country," "Sparrow," "Butterfly Effect"

Gray's Sporting Journal, "Fishing the Little J beneath the Methodist Church"

Janus, "The Handler"

The Journal, "Cracking Coal," "First Light"

Laurel Review, "Counting the Plants," "Leah Tree," "River Vows," "The Yellow House"

Poetry Northwest, "Mock Orange," "Snake Man," "Poem with a Line from Wallace Stevens," "From the Apple Tree," "Astray" (originally published under a different title), "The Car," "Funeral," "My Mother Fished for Carp," "Rabbit Scare"

Quarterly West, "Dirt"

Prairie Schooner, "When My Father Went Out to Shovel Snow"

Salmagundi, "My Mother's Needles," "Dream Catcher"

Shenandoah, "A History," "Summer Spiders"

Tar River Poetry, "My Daughter Gives Me Her Autographed Baseball"

West Branch, "Tripe," "Feed Mill," "Onions," "Shovel," "Laurel Stick"

"Butterfly Effect" was selected by James Tate for *The Best American Poetry 1997*.

"Nails" and "Rabbit Scare" appear in *Gorse Cottage Poems,* a limited-edition book from Banshee Press, edited by Lou McKee.

I would like to thank the following:

The Pennsylvania Council on the Arts for a poetry grant in 1996 that allowed me to complete most of the poems in this book.

Kutztown University and the Professional Development Committee of the Pennsylvania State System of Higher Education for a summer grant in 1998.

Barbara Crooker, Vince Balitas, Frank Allen, Paul Martin, Dan Donaghy, faithful readers all, who looked at *Butterfly Effect* in manuscript and offered valuable suggestions.

And Pattiann Rogers and my editor, Emilie Buchwald, for their insights and advice.

My special thanks to Bruce Weigl for our flyfishing adventures on the trout streams of Pennsylvania, and for all his help with many of the poems in this book.

Butterfly Effect

Judge's Introduction

The poems in *Butterfly Effect,* beautifully accessible first in their finely wrought and thoughtful simplicity, create a second beauty by the subtle and complex way in which they present many worlds as one world, interwoven, interdependent.

Within the realm of this poetry, the real world of physical experience is clearly one with the real world of symbol and myth. The reminiscing voice of the poems introduces and returns more than once to the primal images of fish, bird, snake, bear, snow, river, gardens lost and present, the earth in its most elemental dirt and dust, the sustaining fire and ancient coal of the subterranean. These images, along with the mythic stories they suggest, appear and reappear, intermingling, often taking on the qualities of one another. It is not only a snake that coils, but a swallow is said to be "elegant, / in balance with the coiled universe," ("The Handler") and summer spiders work "coiling something in silk" ("Summer Spiders"). In "My Mother Fished for Carp," "that fish with many bones" possesses the flavor of the earth's mud. This is the same basic earth that in other poems covers the working father's face, that gets in the eyes of the young child, in the lungs of the miners, the ashes out of which the okra grows. A dead pigeon, "its eyes dry and sunken" ("A History"); onions drying, resembling "shrunken skulls, / eyes sewn shut" ("Onions"); the small opening, like an eye itself, in the center of the dream catcher, where you are urged to "Put your eyes close" ("Dream Catcher"); the eye of the swallow reminding the poet of the eye of the snake handler through which he sees God ("The Handler")—all of these are many aspects of the same eye. Throughout the book, connections are established among seemingly disparate phenomena.

Human beings, with their wonder, pain, love, and stories, are always of and among these entities, defining them, yet being identified and known by them as well—fisherman, snake handler, stone breaker, coal miner, daughter, father, mother. The specific characters and events of these poems are sculpted by the real world. They are touching and familiar, and the voice that tells of them is straightforward, honest, respectful; the language unpretentious, never becoming tedious with a sense of its own poetic nature. The themes expressed are as timeless as food and warmth, family light and companionship, belief and quest.

The quest presented in this book is of two kinds: human and non-human alike seek out one another. Humans search, as in "River Vows," for "just the lure of the water, / and what hid underneath," and in "Fishing the Little J beneath the Methodist Church," "I cast long after dark at splashes, / as though I were trying to raise / the spirit of the place." In "Owl Call," blue jays, crows, a fox respond to the sound of the horn-shaped owl call luring them forth, and the owl eventually comes too.

Elements of the universe in turn seek humans. A maple ("Leah Tree"), newly planted, seems to follow the father and his daughter. In "Sparrow," "The fields are blue, / and come at my house like the sea." Snow arrives on its own, "A hint of drifting" ("Ghost Snow"), and the father goes out to meet it, delighting in its presence. "He'd be at it before light," all day "the snow still falling, drifting back to us" ("When My Father Went Out to Shovel Snow"). Even the dead approach. The speaker imagines his absent father walking toward him, trying to come close enough "to allow me to brush dirt off his face" ("The Yellow House"). In "Grizzly Country," the speaker wonders, "What is it we don't hear right away, / . . . so beautiful / one might love its approach?" From the human to the non-human and vice versa, these quests proceed in both directions and become an element unifying variant worlds.

The craft of this poetry itself is unifying. Metaphors are found not only within poems but are sometimes created between two poems. "Feed Mill" concludes with two children standing on a huge, truck-size scale, their weight not sufficient to register at all. Later, in "Ghost Snow," the snow is portrayed as weightless, altering little. This poem ends with the lines,

"Not seethe / or obliteration. / Something / on a lower scale." It is a pleasure to find these two poems functioning together to establish a comparison in a quiet and unobtrusive way, a way exactly suited to the theme of each poem. Another example of this technique occurs between "Dream Catcher" and "Mock Orange." The closing lines of "Dream Catcher"—"a long shot against the world's / night without end"— are recalled in "Mock Orange" when, on his fifty-ninth birthday, the speaker's brother calls to say he has just made twenty consecutive foul shots, "what it means to hit the world / twenty times in a row dead center." No single poem in this book concludes finally with its ending but continues to complete and be completed by other poems in the collection.

Echoing strong images poem to poem, establishing metaphors between poems, repeating certain resonating words throughout the book, these techniques reinforce the poet's desire to present all forces and facts of the world as interrelated, bound to the essences of one another. Ultimately the form of this book itself creates unity, thus becoming not only the source of the melding of worlds but the embodiment of its own vision. The themes and individual poems in *Butterfly Effect* fit together as perfectly and inevitably as polygons in a geodesic dome. They embody a most pleasingly coherent whole, each poem autonomous and bound to its own integrity, yet echoing and supporting the images, music, and credences of each of the others.

Touch one poem and the resulting reverberations can be detected throughout the book, not unlike the results of the swallowtail's movement on the life of the earth in "Butterfly Effect." And over all, Harry Humes's consistent voice works its binding magic in its own cadence—contemplative, full of wonder, grateful, compassionate, "not wanting to scare off anything / that was even for a little while / at rest in my father's garden" ("Rabbit Scare").

PATTIANN ROGERS

Butterfly
Effect

First Light

This time of year I wake early
and go back to the old house,
easing along the south wall,
kicking the foundation, looking up
at the big window I put in,
that looks out over alfalfa and corn,
then kneeling, tasting the ground,
sipping the honeysuckle,
moving across the bridge and porch,
tense as a voyeur as I look
into the kitchen, and remember
us dancing room to room,
laughing, the two little girls shrieking,
holding onto our legs past closets,
the floor with its dry-rotted beams
creaking and sagging, sunlight
or darkness at the front door and back,
my left hand trembling with its dreams
of nailheads and putty,
moving closer to the doorknob,
wanting to be inside
with the two quilts and the sofa,
wanting to sit at the oak table,
waiting for first light over the barn,
swearing never to leave.

Dream Catcher

Just some grape vine braided into a circle,
held fast with twists of wire,

some thread woven across the O,
a small opening in the center

for good dreams to slip through,
all others snagged. Imagine a hand

each morning plucking those
and putting them into a box

kept way back in a dirt cellar.
Imagine that hand adding a feather,

some yellow string, a piece of branch
shaped like a deer's antler.

Or go past all that
to what we most believe,

that we can clear the air,
brighten the corner, watch over children.

Put your eyes close to it.
What happens is a small swaying,

a long shot against the world's
night without end.

From the Apple Tree

Four deer, one with antlers
rubbed smooth against saplings,
eat apples, jaws circling and grinding,
their ears moving constantly,
listening for twig snap,
brush of a sleeve against bark.
I could watch them the rest of my life,
teaching my children how to live
in such light as this,
how to move just so through the world,
how to sit still,
to let nothing get by,
musk glands inside the hind legs,
the swollen curve of the buck's neck,
his antlers dipping
as he sniffs the doe,
branches cool and rough
against my fingers.
Over the pond the dark presses in,
and one deer suddenly balances on hind legs,
front feet tucked under its chest,
head stretched toward some rose-hip berries,
and above it an early star I don't know,
and this need to have the deer
vanish on their own,
not scared away by me,
everything intact, unchanged,
as if I'd not been there at all.

Summer Spiders

It will take a minute, maybe two,
for the black and yellow spiders

to sidle up,
clicking their teeth,

rubbing their legs together,
fixing the small rips in their webs.

We go back and forth
between them and the porch,

watching them dart out
at the web's least tremble.

They know about light and darkness,
and maybe even sorrow.

All of that spinning
among the digitalis and tall yarrow,

all of that living,
that coiling something in silk.

A History

I like pigeons best,
fan tails and tumblers,
their horny legs,
their morning cooing
up on the barn's crossbeam.

Sometime I find one fallen,
its eyes dry and sunken,
its feathers dull,
and I carry it out back for the mice.

Long moments in a long afternoon,
these pigeons are a kind of music,
a history of wind and grit,
shuffling past tomatoes,
nodding over earwigs and grubs,
as if pretending to be wise.

The Car

Windows smashed, seats torn,
hood sprung, one door shotgunned,
axle-deep in leaf rot and topsoil.

Once in the rain I sat behind
the weather-stained steering wheel
that moved beneath my hands,

as did, suddenly, a snake
black as engine oil,
sprawled long and wrist-thick

across the driveshaft
and into the shadows under the seat.
Ferns dripped and sagged.

A wren sat on a limb.
Fog rose from the marsh.
Not a sound anywhere,

not from the flicking tongue,
not from the eyes like wax,
not from the slowly turning head,

nor from the body that rippled,
and took a long time
to slip beneath the floor.

Rabbit Scare

After he put his tomatoes in,
and a row or two of beans,
he pounded a broomstick at each end
and stretched between them a length of twine,
hung from it bottles and tin cans
that clicked and rattled against each other.

But at night, with the wind
off the mountain, they moaned
and kept us under covers.
Just the ghost of some old miner, he'd say,
up and about in the dark,
poor soul, after my tomatoes.

It was years later I blew across
the mouth of a soda bottle
and remembered waking in the dark,
getting up nerve to slip quietly to the window,
not wanting to scare off anything
that was even for a little while
at rest in my father's garden.

Gladiola Man

Each spring he'd plant acres of them,
and not one for sale,
not one given away,
every day weeding, loosening the soil,
fluttering over the spears,
then the big blossoms.
He'd kneel, almost invisible
in the rows where we knew
he was talking to them,
sobbing when wind snapped a stem.

Each October he'd cut them back,
carry the sheaves to the field's edge,
then dig up the bulbs,
gently lift them out,
lay them side by side,
as if he were Leakey at Olduvai Gorge
standing alone at evening,
fitting together dry silence.

Leah Tree

This maple planted yesterday,
lowered into its hole,
set straight, watered,
staked and wired
against the fierce winds over this hill.
This tree I promised you
when you cried inconsolably
about leaving our old house,
its stream and fields,
the overgrown orchard
that you could see from your bedroom.
Now the tree rustles.
We will hang feathers
and sunflower feeders
from its branches.
I wanted to tell you about people,
and about relationships,
branch to bird, bird to air,
old familiar places and new,
blue sky to the blue in your eyes.
We walked as far as the sumac
and looked back.
We could hear it over the grass.
It is following us, you said.
And in low evening light
that is how it seemed.

Butterfly Effect

Think of it in Beijing,
the swallowtail on its white blossom.

Over there a man sleeps
beneath a bo tree.

A woman walks by a pond of red carp.
It is the last of September,

and the sky is clear all the way to the mountains.
No one sees the butterfly's wings move

nor feels the air stir
in the afternoon,

the small disturbance on the pond.
And when the swallowtail flies off

it is just a little more of the same,
a branch creaking, a ripple

over some geography like light over wheat,
except a month later,

thousands of miles away,
a wind knocks trees over,

it snows for days.
Children no longer turn somersaults.

Women turn away from sifting and measuring,
a man watches a deer stagger,

starving, across the frozen river.
The horizon hardly stirs,

and all the pianos are silent.
The bright wing of the sky

drifts so close you could raise a hand
to it, the air delicate

and your fingers itching a little,
as if something had landed there.

River Vows

for Karen and Dan Donaghy

Even in the rain, who would question
the clarity of this day, the plucked notes
of the harpist, and the old chapel itself,
with its four doric columns, big doors,
spare wooden seats, snug and easy
on us as such a place ought to be.
And outside flowed the river,
thick currents, gulls, swirls
of mist against the mountain.

And me suddenly thinking
of the bass and pike out there.
It was nothing of disrespect or boredom,
but, as always, just the lure of the water,
and what hid underneath.
The same with words or love,
or any blink of an eye, in which
something rises, a look, a touch,
and casts over us what is unseen,
irresistible, that we long for all our lives long.

Poem with a Line
from Wallace Stevens

The stream looked lifeless,
as if there'd never been trout
feeding next to a snag, never a snake
leaving a small wake.
As if no one had ever sat on the thick grass
watching water drift through pools.

It was all stabbed by autumn's slanted light,
all the fish-minds stunted,
a season's brilliance of asters and gentian,
butterflies over the tops of willows,
slowly underpowered.

That half-buried bicycle wheel
and sway of weeds,
those red leaves moving just under the surface.

An idleness, a stiffness of shadows
under the footbridge
and where the water bent into the woods.

This distillation of sadness out of a long round
promise.
This return to the plain sense of things.

Keeping Time

It was the best time for him,
when he'd open the Methodist hymnal,
the organ's brass pipes gleaming,
beginning to tremble,
my father up from his mine tunnels,
coal dirt deep in his skin,
wearing his good suit,
impatient for the minister
to ask us to rise, my father
patting his coat pocket,
clearing his throat.
I'd stare at the window
where Jesus
knelt among lambs,
until at first low,
then gathering volume
on each word, my father's voice,
rose off-key above all others,
and not a soul staring
at his swaying,
at his right hand back and forth,
at his deep gulps of air,
loosening his necktie,
lost to us,
keeping time in his own sweet way.

Fishing the Little J
beneath the Methodist Church

for Bruce Weigl and Bob Haas

I stand upstream with the spire
and stained glass of the white church
over my shoulder as when I was a boy
in that coal town trailing my string
through silted-up mine water,
thinking of my father's Sunday morning voice,
and my mother's hands crossed in her lap,
the sermon flow and choir.

Now my white fly
with wings of mandarin feathers,
belly of red fox fur and tail of ginger quill
quarters across the current
toward the overhang of willows
where a trout has been feeding,
and then to another in a swirl behind rock,
the light growing less, until

with the push of current against my legs,
my hands cold, I hear a faint music
over the water, and for a while
I'm uncertain of where I am,
what I am doing,
or for what reason
I cast long after dark at splashes,
as though I were trying to raise
the spirit of this place,
one fish of such heft
that my life would be forever after
set in the arc of its power.

Ax Heads

Handles shattered, our father
would carry them home from his mine,
and next day build a fire,
let us pile on branches until it roared.
In went the ax heads,
flames and sparks shooting out,
and him off to cut new handles,
leaving us to make sure
the whole place didn't go up.
When he came back, he'd drag them out
with a wire hanger and douse them,
telling us they'd be just grand.
He'd whittle the handle ends,
tap the heads down, and drive in a shim,
holding one out for each of us,
asking about balance and feel,
saying they were the same
as if the priest himself
had blessed them
against ever shattering again,
and us nodding, happy with him,
and then standing well back
as he tested each one,
splitting big rounds of apple and oak,
their sharp scent and glistening white
like storms driven close.

Owl Call

I found it hanging on a cellar nail
where my father put it twenty years before.
Black, shaped like a little horn,
a piece of cord tied around it,
it moaned through the cellar
and up the steps into the kitchen.
I took it into the woods
and sat against a tree.
Bluejays came in when I called,
crows mobbed the tops of trees,
filling the woods with their cries.
A fox barked once and slipped away,
its tail straight out,
its feet neatly in a line.
Then the owl came in,
landed on the pine,
ear tufts and finger-long talons,
tomcat head turning,
buoyant and silent when it swooped,
yellow eyes coming softly
at my eyes, swerving away and flaring up
to a branch where it swayed
side to side, feathers puffed out,
clicking its beak,
and me with the call halfway to my lips,
wanting to say something else.

Grizzly Country

Before she crawled into her sleeping bag,
she ate a cold supper,
had no small fire for comfort,
hoisted her pack into a tree,
did not wash her hands or face,
did not hum or whistle.

The bear found her anyway,
came quietly down some scree,
crossed the stream,
and took her out of the tent.

This evening, only a few hours past
the winter solstice, I wonder
where I was when the bear lifted
its snout into the sky.
Did I look at first snow over Hawk Mountain?
Or at my daughter?
Did I hear something beyond the blue spruce?

What is it goes wrong with our knowing?
What is it we don't hear right away,
or ever, that comes fully grown,
silver guard hair brilliant on its shoulders,
not clumsy, but stunning
in its moves, so beautiful
one might love its approach?

Astray

Who are you? she'd ask,
squinting, leaning toward me,
pushing her glasses back
the way she did.
Her hair wavy and gray,
knees together,
her hands calm in her lap,
hands that had taken a butcher knife
to chase her husband around the house,
cursing his pipe smoke in every room,
cursing that she'd had to turn Catholic,
go to mass and confession,
leave her sisters behind
in the Methodist church
to live lonely in the railroad town
along the river.
She'd only nicked
his shoulder and wrist
before she forgot what she was doing,
walked outside, took off her clothes,
and fell asleep on the grass.
Asking me again my name,
Was I Irish? Did I smoke?
Then brushing back my hair,
saying *Harry, Harry,*
and a minute later
asking who I was
and what was I doing in that house.

Counting the Plants

Habanero, cayenne, tomatillo tomatoes,
late cabbage, zucchini, some beans
a dozen willowy asparagus,

the sundial at the center
of lamb's ear and yarrow and dill.
I think of okra my father grew in ashes

mixed with pigeon droppings,
okra that my mother fried crisp and brown.
Waiting for supper, his face mine-black,

he never imagined a place like this.
Now with his slow hand
he tries to catch a fly,

asks why I have no okra
in my garden, saying how hungry
he is for a plateful.

Swimming

Maybe she'd be up to her wrists in flour,
or plucking a chicken,
brushing feathers from her face.
Next thing she'd be telling me,
as always, to stay away
from those water-filled mine holes,
their bottoms ready to fall out,
taking you down to who knows where.

Then straight off I'd go
to one of those deep places,
not caring about sunken cables,
corrugated iron, sharp rocks,
not thinking of being caught
in some suck of water.

Nor what I'd have to face later
when she'd pat my almost-dry hair,
smelling it, looking at me,
at the dead giveaway of my blue lips,
that she'd wonder about,
asking if I'd been eating huckleberries,
and her smiling, scratching the red
splotches of eczema on her fingers,
ready to question me again.

Tripe

The woman behind the counter
smiled sweetly, but knew right off
I was not the one for tripe.
I almost expected her to say,
now your old man,
there was a coal-mining tripe eater.
So to show her I was his son,
I pointed to a thick piece and said wrap it up.
Walking home, I felt it shift
in the bag as if alive,
and remembered it on his plate,
slippery, white with horse radish.
It was years before I knew what it was.
I put the tripe
in the refrigerator,
and in four days it turned to slime,
yellow and dripping.
When I took it out to the garbage,
I had to smile at my wife and small daughter,
at my father not yet coughing blood,
holding out his empty plate,
lifting his eyes to heaven.

Dirt Cellar

Crowbars, rakes, picks, barrels of nails,
a thick coat of coal dust on everything.
Always cool and damp, always night,
it could have been a tunnel.
Ceiling beams creaked.
It stank of lye and whitewash.
Years for us to leave it,
to let the bats hang in peace,
and the water and mine gas seep in.
We took a chisel, a saw, a level,
a baseball glove, a box of fossils,
ferns, dried marigolds.
We took the small blue scars
and a little dirt in our lungs.
We left the gloom and the sadness,
the old miners leaning against porches,
trying to catch their breath,
their tongues like the bellies of toads.
We left it,
as if we never believed,
and for so long.

Onions

In August I pull them out
and tie them in rows
along the low branches
of maple trees to dry.
They rustle and sway.
Finch peck them,
my daughter taps them with a stick.
They look like shrunken skulls,
eyes sewn shut like the eye
of my sister before she was thirty,
coming home with her head bandaged,
holding the two daughters
she never dreamed she'd only half see,
hungry, she said.

By late October I cut them down,
their feathery translucent skins
coming off in my hands.
No matter what I do,
chill them, hold them under water
as I slice or chop,
I have to turn away,
rub my eyes, blink it all back.

The Fall

My father made the U-turn
his usual slow way at Sweeney's corner,

beeped at the loafers at Andy's gas station.
Suddenly my door unlatched, swung open.

My father's hand shot out
as I tumbled over the macadam,

the curb, the brick sidewalk,
sitting up, unhurt, laughing,

my father running toward me,
his face red, shouting

What was I doing, falling out like that?
checking me for broken bones,

for blood, telling the loafers to mind
their own goddamned business,

then slumping next to me,
holding the arm he had just missed.

The Handler

What was it about that swallow,
its long narrow pointed wings
sharp against lead-colored clouds?

It caught the wind, stalled,
dropped behind the pin oak, rose again.
And why just then should I have thought

of a man who came to my childhood home,
and while handling a poisonous snake,
told us he saw God?

It was the bird's eye, I think,
the wind that rattled over leaves,
the iridescent green and rust feathers,

deeply notched tail,
and the feet delicate as spider webs
tucked up beneath the white belly.

Nor have I forgotten
how fierce the bird was, and elegant,
in balance with the coiled universe.

Snake Man

Brown and late autumn gray,
it climbed up his arm
looking for heat,
for the screech owl
the man had held earlier.
Nervous, edgy, a little dangerous,
its eyes never wavered,
and when the triangular head,
pits and glands and fangs
in their soft sacs,
reached above the elbow,
the man slid his stick
gently beneath its middle,
and it draped there like a necktie.
When he held it out,
I touched it,
felt the delicate ribs,
the rattles stuck together like toys.
The tongue flicked
over my wrist,
and then the mouth
with its dry smile
turned slowly toward some movement
in the afternoon,
away to the stone fences,
the mountains miles away.

Laurel Stick

After it was cut and dried,
my father scraped
and trimmed the branches,
cut back its length,
shaped the knobby handle.
You'll never find a straight laurel,
he said, holding up the twisted stick.

Tonight I found it wrapped
in a burlap bag way back in a closet.
I sighted along its curves,
felt the laurel's heft,
the handle scratched and worn,
and the tip nicked
from when he'd punch
through a puddle's ice
or bat a stone
over our back fence. Balancing
the stick at my side, I leaned,
trusting a new way to walk.

My Daughter Gives Me
Her Autographed Baseball

And I take it, rolling it in my hands.
It is my birthday. She is so happy
when we read aloud the players' names.
I curl my fingers over the red stitching,
the white leather warm against my palm,
remembering the dirt field,
the blue scar on my knee from sliding,
the ball we used, cover long worn off,
covered again and again
with black electrician's tape.

This way, I show her once more,
imagining the ball cutting the air,
then curving down and away,
as between us the curve
of our moment falls so slow and easy
I think it will last forever.

Mock Orange

On his fifty-ninth birthday,
my brother calls to say he'd just sunk
twenty foul shots in a row,
the old way, underhanded,
not one touching the rim.
It was the old groove, he said,
rolling the ball between his fingers,
not even feeling his feet against the boards.
Twenty in a row, he says again,
and then nothing else,
not whether he'd gone for a beer,
or thought of our mother's mock orange bush,
its heavy sweet scent all through June,
those big white blossoms
we'd collect after they'd dropped,
putting them into our pockets,
thinking they'd become real oranges,
watching them brown and curl.
In the silence I want to tell him
I'd found one in the woods,
and carried a few shoots back to my house,
wondering why I did not say it,
trying to remember, after we hang up,
what it means to hit the world
twenty times in a row dead center.

The Yellow House

My father would love it here,
waking before dawn to coffee or black tea,
a raw egg on the screened-in porch,
brushing mosquitos away,
then waving goodbye, goodbye,
doing the five-step
from when he was a boy,
his socks rolled around his ankles.
He'd whistle along the path toward the fishing
    boats,
lighthouse and the purple martens,
down over the mud flats,
throwing chicken necks to the crabs,
and walk as far as the wild ponies.
It's hard to say if he would spend an hour
with the honeysuckle and yarrow stalks,
or with the whirlpools beneath the bridge,
or with the herons, their reptilian necks
and fierce eyes, long beaks
full of small fish.
He'd have time to go as far
as the high dunes,
and when he came back he'd recognize me,
as he tried to hide his cough,
the coal-streaked phlegm,
waving, trying to come close,
to allow me to brush dirt off his face.

Dirt

I was told I'd have to eat
a peck before I died,
and me wondering how big was a peck
and if I'd have a big belly
like the men at Lavelle's Bar.
Some nights in our valley
were so dirty-dark
you'd think someone had shaken
out a rug at a back door
and that you'd need only
to open your mouth
to take in a year's worth
and be well along toward dying.
I always kept my lips tight
when I ran to the store
for summer sausage and bread
for my father's lunch.
There was dirt in his lungs
from the tunnels where he worked.
When he'd cough,
his spit was darkly streaked.
Once a gust blew into my eyes,
so I had to feel my way home,
wall by wall, telephone pole
by telephone pole,
crying back to our kitchen
where my mother twisted the corner
of her handkerchief,
wet it in her mouth,

then dug it into my eyes,
telling me not to wiggle,
Jesus, Mary, and Joseph,
it was only dirt, wasn't it?
There was worse waiting for me.

Feed Mill

high as a church,
homely as a house.

—Elizabeth Bishop, "The Moose"

Everything gray or grayish brown
in the light drifting
through cracks in walls,
down over barrels, long-handled scoops,
conveyer belts, piles of burlap bags,
bone meal, fertilizer, lime,
gears rumbling and grinding,
men in boots and heavy coats
appearing up out of trapdoors
or disappearing around corners,
coughing in dusty air.

And our father doing what he always did
those Saturday mornings,
buying feed for his pigeons,
lifting heavy sacks
of cracked corn and millet
up on his shoulders,
telling us to run ahead
and open the car,
and us asking to see the scales,
their lead weights, needles, hooks,
unsteady when we stepped up on them,
and one big as a truck
that registered nothing,
as if we were not even skin and bones.

Cracking Coal

Lumps big as basketballs all around him,
a ball-peen hammer in his hand,
he'd strike straight along the grain,
sharp pieces flying off,
nicking his arms, glancing off his glasses.

Sitting there the whole afternoon,
face dirty, gloves worn through,
until he had broken the pile into pieces
the size of chestnuts or peas.

He'd fill the outside bin,
and rattle a bucketful
over the blue flames of the fire box,
then lift us high
to let us spit on the stove,
that sizzle disappearing.

My mother shaking her head,
all of us there in late afternoon,
snow just beginning
over rooftops and pigeon coops,
a little sulphur in the air.

My Mother Fished for Carp

Off she'd go at first light,
hooks, rod, dough bait wrapped in waxed
    paper,
walking five miles to the murky pond,
casting, sitting still for hours
for what sucked and burrowed
along the bottom, those thick-bodied fish
with hard-ringed mouths,
scales big as nickels,
sides red-slashed, bubbles rising
in their wake, smell of swamp gas,
and then suddenly the bobber moving,
pulled under, my mother feeding out line,
then striking up and back,
a big fish she carried back to us,
reading our fortunes in its blood,
telling us we would marry,
live with children in small houses,
and have troubles all our own.
We each touched the fish
before it was wrapped
in foil and baked all afternoon,
that fish with many bones,
that tasted of mud,
over which she said our grace.

Ghost Snow

Almost not there against
the side of the red barn,
almost not ticking dry leaves.
Not a hint of wind.
A stillness.
An easing of edges.
Already the path
less worn
past cinquefoil
and snakeweed stalks.
Finch and siskin hunch
on sumac branches,
feet curled under,
feathers plumped.
A hint of drifting
in the old orchard,
over deadfalls and crannies,
and over the little hill
where each spring
bloodroot rise.
Not seethe
or obliteration.
Something
on a lower scale.

Shovel

Black tape low on the long handle
where the rivets come through,
a crack out from under the tape,
the word *Hook* carved just above there,
and the spade bent
from my father banging it against rock
and coal at Packer 5.
Once each spring he'd carry it home
to dig his tomato and potato patch,
loosening it wedge by wedge,
setting in the little eyes
and leggy plants.
When I take it from the shed wall,
I like its feel, the years of its balance,
the length of it cocked in my hands
as it must have in the miner's hands,
his carbide lamp hissing in the pitch black
under the mountain.
This snow hissing and blowing
over my neighbor's barn,
and two crows on the mulch pile
digging into orange peels,
frozen crusts of dark bread.

Sparrow

I find the sparrow on its side,
feathers fluffed by wind, eyes glazed.

The fields are blue,
and come at my house like the sea.

There's a purple low down in the west.
Snow drifts off my neighbor's barn

like the plume of a great peak.
The sparrow has a white bib,

its feet delicate, curled like spiders.
Last night was the coldest night

of the year, and cloudless,
but the sparrow is not dead.

We touch its brown head,
It sits on the kitchen table

and on our fingers.
We huddle around its small fire.

Sleet Crow

All beak, shining and lumpish in the maple,
waiting for windows to be free of movement.

Farther off in the hickory, three others sit.
I put out corn and sunflower seeds,

dry bread, peanut butter hearts.
The crow hops to a lower limb,

rocks forward and back
in an opening into the tree

I have never seen.
It wants to land on the corn.

It strokes its beak against a limb.
On its neck a little snow.

It could kill and eat the juncos and finch.
A midnight of resurrection,

it is the end of branches,
tick of sleet against dry leaves.

Nails

Buckets of them, rusted or shining,
spikes and tar paper nails, five-penny and ten,
pocketsful he'd bring home from his mine,
spilling them out over the oilcloth
on the kitchen table, smiling,
pleased with his petty thievery,
something else he could carry back to us
along with dust in his lungs and bad legs.

Sometimes I'd drive them
into trees or the ground,
and once tried to count them,
my hands nicked and bleeding.
They went into dog pens and pigeon coops.
We threw them at bottles,
or slingshot them at rats and birds.
All that time those nails keeping our house
and its troubles from drifting off.

Funeral

Drunk, an older brother
burst into our living room,
pushed aside the preacher,
cursed, waved his arms,
lurched against the coffin,
and knocked it over.
My Uncle Nate's body
in good suit and black shoes
rolled onto the floor,
rocked once and settled.
I held my breath,
forced back laughter,
while the undertaker's white hands
eased my uncle back into place,
straightening flowers,
patting down clothes and hair.
My mother raised her eyes
to heaven and moaned,
as the screaming brother
was dragged through the kitchen,
down twenty-five porch steps
into our backyard,
slapped, kicked, warned,
and thrown into the alley.
When I went out hours later,
he was still there,
coat sleeve torn off,
somehow sadder than the coffin,
waving me close
with his dirty, crushed hat,
weeping, mumbling through bloody lips
something like love.

When My Father Went Out
to Shovel Snow

He'd be at it before light,
his big scoop scraping through the crust,
piling it up around the telephone pole,
working his way to the DeSoto,
then clearing a path down our backyard,
all morning the snow falling
and him out there,
clearing what he'd already cleared,
coming in only for a cup of coffee,
telling my mother, *It's great, great,*
saying she ought to pull on some boots
and try it, then out again,
his big scoop flashing all afternoon,
until he'd come in for supper,
sipping black tea from his saucer,
cutting the end from a loaf of bread,
his boots still on,
gloves drying on the stove.
Look at it, he'd say,
patting my mother's hand,
the snow still falling, drifting back to us.

My Mother's Needles

Sitting in her chair that faced away
from the window, she'd ask,
"I wonder if you could thread a few for me."
And so we'd stay together an afternoon,
her with her milky eyes, remembering
picnics, drives in the DeSoto,
her garden of sage and parsley,
the double mock orange bush
and black cherry.
And me wetting the end
of thread, rolling it to a point
between my fingertips, then easing it
through the eye, drawing the ends down even.
As always she'd say, "Now don't knot them."
Hours like that, easy, away from things.
I'd stick a dozen along the arms
of her chair where she could reach out
for one, still ready for a little mending,
the miner's work clothes, her boys' shirts
out at the elbows, and her hardly able
to get a seam straight or keep
a patch flat across the middle.
All the way home I'd see her
leaning forward in the chair,
telling me something else she'd just
then thought of, her hands fluttering,
voice still sharp, stitching it all together.

HARRY HUMES's most recent books of poetry are *Gorse Cottage Poems* (Banshee Press, 1998) and *The Bottomland* (University of Arkansas Press, 1995). His first book of poems, *Winter Weeds,* was the Devins Award selection for 1983 (University of Missouri, 1983). He is the recipient of a National Endowment for the Arts Poetry Fellowship and several Pennsylvania Council on the Arts poetry grants. *Poetry Northwest* awarded him its Theodore Roethke Poetry Award, and his poem "Butterfly Effect," originally published in the *Gettysburg Review,* was selected by James Tate for *The Best American Poetry of 1997.*

More poetry from Milkweed Editions

To order books or for more information,
contact Milkweed at (800) 520-6455 or visit our
website (www.milkweed.org).

Outsiders:
Poems about Rebels, Exiles, and Renegades
Edited by Laure-Anne Bosselaar

Drive, They Said:
Poems about Americans and Their Cars
Edited by Kurt Brown

Night Out:
Poems about Hotels, Motels, Restaurants, and Bars
Edited by Kurt Brown and
Laure-Anne Bosselaar

Verse and Universe:
Poems about Science and Mathematics
Edited by Kurt Brown

Astonishing World:
Selected Poems of Ángel González
Translated from the Spanish by
Steven Ford Brown

Mixed Voices:
Contemporary Poems about Music
Edited by Emilie Buchwald and Ruth Roston

This Sporting Life:
Poems about Sports and Games
Edited by Emilie Buchwald and Ruth Roston

Eating the Sting
John Caddy

The Phoenix Gone, The Terrace Empty
Marilyn Chin

Twin Sons of Different Mirrors
Jack Driscoll and Bill Meissner

Invisible Horses
Patricia Goedicke

The Art of Writing:
Lu Chi's Wen Fu
Translated from the Chinese by Sam Hamill

Boxelder Bug Variations
Bill Holm

The Dead Get By with Everything
Bill Holm

The Freedom of History
Jim Moore

The Long Experience of Love
Jim Moore

Minnesota Writes:
Poetry
Edited by Jim Moore and Cary Waterman

Eating Bread and Honey
Pattiann Rogers

Firekeeper:
New and Selected Poems
Pattiann Rogers

White Flash/Black Rain:
Women of Japan Relive the Bomb
Edited by Lequita Vance-Watkins
and Aratani Mariko

Milkweed Editions publishes with the intention of making a humane impact on society, in the belief that literature is a transformative art uniquely able to convey the essential experiences of the human heart and spirit.

To that end, Milkweed publishes distinctive voices of literary merit in handsomely designed, visually dynamic books, exploring the ethical, cultural, and esthetic issues that free societies need continually to address.

Milkweed Editions is a not-for-profit press.

Interior design by Donna Burch
Typeset in Sabon
by Stanton Publication Services, Inc.
Printed on acid-free Glatfelter paper
by Bang Printing